LIFE

"I'm still working on it"

ARTHUR LUKE

has **'if '** in it for a reason - so make it count

ARTHUR LUKE

First edition June 2018 | Published by Arthur Luke

Cover design: Arthur Luke - www.arthurluke.co.uk
Cover photography: Camila Damásio - Salvador, Brazil - www.miladamasio.com
Edited by: The wonderful - Jenni Doig and Molly Luke
Illustrations on pages 36 and 206 by the amazing Hilary Pearson

To Hilary - my best friend, who has saved me from myself too many times to mention;

to my daughters Molly and Tess, your life is your life - 'you the man'.

To the memory of Paul Winyard

1955 - 2009

We shared part of the journey together, it was a wild and rocky ride of excess. We never questioned it, we just did it and tried to survive.

If you can dream - and not make dreams your master,

If you can think - and not make thoughts your aim;

If you can meet with Triumph and Disaster

And treat those two impostors just the same;

If you can bear to hear the truth you've spoken

Twisted by knaves to make a trap for fools,

Or watch the things you gave your life to, broken,

And stoop and build 'em up with worn-out tools:

... If you can fill the unforgiving minute

With sixty seconds' worth of distance run,

Yours is the Earth and everything that's in it,

And - which is more - you'll be a Man, my son!

Extract from 'IF' by Rudyard Kipling (1865-1936)

Who am I?

If I'm honest, and that's the whole point of this book - I'm a pessimist who lives life like an optimist. I'm a glass-half-empty guy with a glass-full of determination.

I've tasted success and failure in frustratingly equal measure and although my body says I'm 62 my heart tells me I'm 16 with a whole lot still to learn.

I have a level of stubbornness and self-drive that dominates my acute shyness and lack of self-confidence. I'm two complete opposites inhabiting the same body.

At one point in my life, I was three people with three very successful careers all at the same time (more on that later).

But, this book is not about me (ok, maybe some of it is), it's about what I've learned along the way, and I hope it helps you fight whatever may be stopping you stopping 'you' from reaching your full potential.

"The person who doesn't scatter the morning dew will not comb grey hairs."

Hunter S. Thompson

Contents

Do you want the good news or the bad news first?

The bad news is:

Very few of us get to do exactly what we want in life. 'Life and work', or in most cases 'work and life', get in the way.

Things haven't changed much since our parents were young in that we still 'live to work to live'.

Most (but not all) of us hate Mondays, long for Fridays and, as the years go by, slowly commute our way to retirement or death, whichever comes first.

"If today were the last day of my life, would I want to do what I am about to do today?" – Steve Jobs

ARTHUR LUKE

The good news is:

It doesn't have to be that way.

Whether you're a university graduate, a senior manager, have just been made redundant, just retired, a mother of three with a mortgage *(and can't remember the last time you had any time to yourself)*, or you're just in a dead end job and you're desperate to break free from the 9 to 5, you can change your life to the way you want it to be.

I'm not saying it's easy and if my journey is anything to go by it won't be, but it's the only way to fly.

Remember: You're never too young, too old, or too late to do something new.

What life has taught me so far!

Age does not guarantee wisdom. Old souls do inhabit young bodies. I've met many amazing young people wise beyond their tender years. I've listened to teenagers voice pearls of wisdom I could never hope to match.

"Age is foolish and forgetful when it underestimates youth" - J.K.Rowling.

Age is, without doubt, less a state of mind and more about the state of your body.

When I look in the mirror, I don't see 62-year-old me, but when I bend down, I remember that I am.

So my advice to anyone reading this book *(thank you by the way)* is - if you wait, all that happens is you get older.

LIFE

Whatever path you choose and whoever you are, life is still: limited to (one) per person: subject to change without notice; non-negotiable or transferable; provided "as is" and without warranties; may incur damages from use or misuse; available for a limited time only; subject to terms and conditions.

*Note: Mileage may vary. Additional parts sold separately. Other as yet unknown restrictions may come into force at any time.

*Warning: The owner will be subject to tax and other fees where applicable (usually as much as your government can get away with).

What I would tell 20 year old me!

As I enter my 63rd year of life I wish I had realised the following *(in no particular order)*:

1. Never be afraid to start, you must start today, now!

2. Most things in life are a matter of perspective. The moment you change your perspective, you become a different person.

3. Do something you love and are passionate about. Sadly most (but not all of us) don't.

4. Always jump in at the deep end.

5. Don't make someone a priority, when you are just an option to them.

6. Read. Then read more and more and more...

7. Stop watching the TV. Apparently the average person watches over nine years of TV and you can bet most of it will be repeats!

8. Think hard about taking that 9 to 5 job unless it is a stepping stone to starting your own business. After all who wants to have to ask their boss if they can go to the toilet!

ARTHUR LUKE

9. Trust people until they give you a reason not to.

10. Entrepreneurs are no different to anyone else. You don't set out to be an entrepreneur, it happens along the way. They don't have magic powers – they are just like you. The only difference is they don't just dream it, they do it.

11. Say no. Half of the troubles of this life can be traced to saying yes too quickly and not saying no soon enough.

12. Ask more questions.

13. Visit Mum and Dad more often - this one is to my own children :)

14. Be patient. There's no advantage to rushing through life *"All great achievements require time."* – Maya Angelou

15. People will try to discourage you. Don't let them. Believe in yourself and don't worry about what other people think.

16. Don't compare yourself to others. Focus on your own game.

17. Everything is figureoutable (if that's even a word).

LIFE - Optimism

The pessimist complains about the wind; the optimist expects it to change; the realist adjusts the sails.

- William Arthur Ward

OPTIM**IS**M

A 6 INCH PENCIL WITH ONLY A QUARTER INCH ERASER

When I was a child I loved starting a new empty notebook *(still do)*. It was full of possibilities. Ideas I had yet to imagine. Stories I had yet to write and pictures I had still to draw.

The first clean new empty page was always the hardest to start.

What if I made a mistake? What if it was rubbish?

That first page held so much pressure, so much risk.

The future of my new notebook was in the balance: one false start, and it would be ruined.

I'm not sure if I should even tell you this, but sometimes I would sit there looking at that first - page paralysed. The pessimist in me would not let me pick up my pencil. At the same time, the optimist in me was on the edge of my seat desperate to create.

Looking back on it now it's like starting anything new, you have to jump right in and see what happens.

If you ruin the first page, there are plenty of fresh ones right behind it.

So be an optimist - *"at least until they start moving animals in pairs to Cape Canaveral"* - Anon

ARTHUR LUKE

When two dogs go to war

*A Native American Indian once described his inner struggle as two dogs, one a pessimist and the other an optimist. 'The pessimist is always fighting the optimist,' he said. When asked which dog wins, he thought for a moment and then replied, 'The one I decide to feed.'

The truth is - we all have those two dogs - it is up to you which one you feed today.

By the way, mine are both rottweilers most of the time - what are yours?

'You'
are more talented
than you think!

'You' are more talented than you think.

I've talked to many people over the years who have had no idea what they were good at.

They believed they had no discernible talents at all when, in fact, we all have infinite gifts; we just haven't discovered them all yet.

To find these talents all you need is a little curiosity, some courage, and a hunger to break free from the limitations and expectations put on us by others and ourselves.

Unfortunately, society encourages conformity. Parents don't want you to take risks because they love you, employers want you to help them achieve their goals, not yours, and the education system *(at the mercy of whatever government is in power)* often seems driven by results rather than helping students discover their talents.

Add to that the 'fear of the new' most of us suffer from, and we have a recipe for 'life paralysis' and bad decisions.

In the end, it is down to you to find where your real talents lie!

Success has little to do with education; it's about self-discipline, a willingness to learn, the ability to keep going when things get tough, stubborn determination and a spoonful of lady luck.

When I was at school, I was repeatedly discouraged from studying art. My teachers thought I would never be any good at it and the school agreed *(they nearly had me believing it too)*.

They recommended I got an apprenticeship in the shipyards which I foolishly did *(because I thought they knew better)*, thus wasting the next three years of my life *(looking back it was part of a journey that made me who I am today. Nothing is a waste of time if you learn something from it - it's all experience)*.

I later studied art at night school and went on to become creative director of one of the world's biggest branding agencies.

So, what did they know?

Never let the limitations of others limit you.

"Nature has concealed at the bottom of our minds talents and abilities of which we are not aware." - Francois de la Rochefoucauld

"The optimist sees the rose and not its thorns; the pessimist stares at the thorns, oblivious to the rose." - Kahlil Gibran

WHY NOT?

Say it when you're young, and it usually gets you into trouble.

Say it at work, and people think you're being difficult.

Say it to yourself, and anything is possible.

So start asking yourself - why the hell not? - why not me? - why not now?

'Why not' is your doorway to the possible - so keep asking until the day you die!

"Some look at things that are, and ask why. I dream of things that never were and ask why not?" - George Bernard Shaw

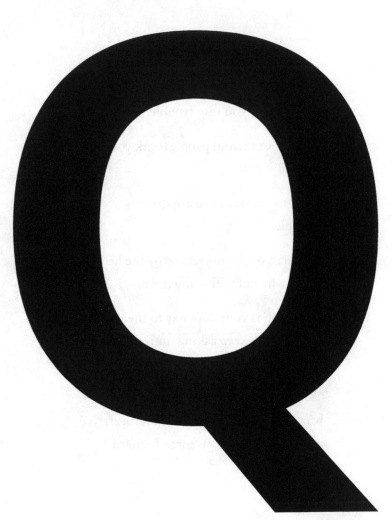

1

Life - does it happen to you, or do you happen to it?

Do you feel powerless or do you feel empowered?

Do you feel in control or out of control?

Do you feel that what happens to you is up to you or is it going to happen anyway?

Do you have a choice or no choice?

I've always believed that life doesn't happen to you; you happen to life. Even writing it down now, on this page, gives me a rush of excitement and optimism! *(calm down Arthur, it's only page 33).*

"You are not a piece of laundry flapping in the breeze. You have to choose to be the cause rather than the effect. You have to decide to make something happen." - Daniel R Castro

Now that is worth getting out of bed for!

On bad days I see opportunities as problems and problems as disasters *(about to happen any minute now).*

On good days I always see problems as opportunities *(a solution misunderstood)* and I can't wait to get started.

Most of the time what turns my good day into a bad one is 'me'.

The truth is that most of the time what stops us *(and me)* from being who we want to be and doing what we want to do - is ourselves!

"When you're having a bad day all you have to do is look at a kettle. It even manages to sing when up to its neck in hot water." - Anon

You can either see problems or opportunities - it's up to you.

ARTHUR LUKE

It never abandons you - you abandon it

When the world says, 'Give up', Hope whispers 'Try it one more time'.

I started my first business at the age of 11 and my most recent at the age of 60. Some were very successful, and many failed so miserably I can't bring myself to tell you what they were.

When I look back they didn't fail because they were bad ideas, they failed because I let self-doubt defeat me first and I had abandoned hope.

Thomas Edison once said, *"Many of life's failures are people who did not realise how close they were to success when they gave up."*

I see hope as a place where possibilities live, and dreams grow.

Never give up on it because without hope we will never find the answers.

ARTHUR LUKE

GENIUS

It's in us all

We all have hidden talents, sadly
too many of us never find them.
Either because we don't believe in
ourselves, or because we don't know
how to tap into them, or others have
convinced us we don't have them, and
our education system isn't set up to
nurture genius.

How many times have you seen that
spark of genius, some hidden talent,
in someone you know?

Maybe today is a good day to remind
someone you know.

ARTHUR LUKE

Embrace uncertainty – it's the door to the unknown

We live in uncertain times and uncertainty is unsettling.

We prefer the familiar, the safe, the predictable and that is perfectly understandable, but that's not easy (or even possible) in a fast-changing world.

Perhaps the safest route to take is to embrace uncertainty. Step into the unknown on your terms.

Don't be a hostage to the actions of others, especially complete strangers.

Don't be scared.

Get out there, do what it is 'you' want to do and see what happens.

Be a daydream believer

When I was young, my mother used to say I was just a dreamer and it was NOT meant as a compliment.

When I was at school, I often got into trouble for staring out of the window. The teacher would say I was just a 'good - for - nothing dreamer; it was NOT meant as a compliment.

They were right I am, but they were wrong in thinking it was a bad thing.

"If a little dreaming is dangerous, the cure for it is not to dream less but to dream more, to dream all the time." – Marcel Proust

Being a dreamer is a good thing, not something to be ashamed of.

"At first, dreams seem impossible, then improbable, and eventually inevitable." – Christopher Reeve

Dreams inspire us. They challenge us, they encourage us, and they give us a glimpse of what is possible. Without them we have nothing.

What's the purpose of life if you don't go after your dreams?

Be a dreamer - but not just a dreamer.

Daydreaming your life away without taking any action is never going to work. One needs the other.

When I was about 12 years old, I was what they called a 'latch-key kid'. Both my parents worked long hours every day and as there was no one at home after school I would go round to my Nanas house for tea.

My grandad was always sitting at the kitchen table (I don't remember him doing anything else), one leg continually shaking under the table. It was some sort of muscle spasm, but I used to think it was a sign that he desperately wanted to escape, but he never did.

He would sit there staring out of the window, day in day out, and when I sat down with him his favourite topic of conversation was "when I win the lottery I will …".

He had been saying it for as long as I could remember and of course, he died without doing any of them.

There's a great line in one of the Harry Potter movies in which Dumbledore catches Harry sitting in front of the 'Mirror of Erised' and in answer to Harry's questions Dumbledore replies: *"It does not do to dwell on dreams and forget to live."*

Be a dreamer but not just a dreamer; you also have to be a doer.

LIFE - Limitations

"We all have our limitations, but when we listen to our critics, we also have theirs." - Robert Brault

Don't be limited by the limitations of others

It's important to know when NOT to seek the advice of others.

Starting something new (which for me is usually an idea for a new business or product) is a step into the unknown. It can be unsettling and frightening – we don't know what the outcome will be.

That first step is often the most difficult, but unless you take it, you're not going anywhere. Your idea will stay an idea, your dream will stay a dream, and the world will be none the wiser.

This can be made more difficult by the limitations of the very friends and colleagues from whom you seek encouragement and validation.

Your new ideas need protection, not because someone might steal them but because well-intentioned feedback can be destructive.

There are countless examples of successful artists, musicians, authors, entrepreneurs and inventors who, if they had listened to others at the very beginning, would never have succeeded.

Yes, you're going to need encouragement and emotional support as you progress, but do some groundwork first.

"Everybody is too busy with their own lives to give a damn about

your book, painting, screenplay, etc., especially if you haven't finished it yet. And the ones who aren't too busy you don't want in your life anyway." – Hugh MacLeod

I used to seek validation from friends about every new business idea I had in mind. I don't anymore.

Coming up with a great idea is a moment of magic, but it is an extremely fragile one.

As is my nature I dive into everything headfirst, with boundless enthusiasm and wearing my heart on my sleeve; I am no different now at 62 than I was at 11.

But new ideas do need protection, and your new embryonic idea needs protection from the limitations of others – especially your friends and family.

I have one friend who when called for encouragement or feedback on a new idea would invariably say: "Oh, I had that idea years ago"; or "I read about another company who've already done that"; or "loads of people have had that idea".

She would then spend 20 minutes telling me how she would do it (interestingly she never realised any of the ideas she came up with but "I could have if I'd wanted to" she would say.)

At first, the result was, I would come away from each call feeling deflated and depressed.

Later I would come away from those calls thinking to myself "Well **** her; I'm doing it anyway".

Now I don't ask anymore. Not only was my idea not ready for harsh criticism, neither was I.

Remember, most of your friends and family have never tried to start a business themselves (or do anything outside the norm).

They also don't want you to fail, they don't want you to take unnecessary risks, they don't want you to make a fool of yourself, and in doing so, they can't see the light for the darkness.

Some people are also, by nature, filled with negativity; they can demolish your fragile beliefs and fill you with doubt. Recognise these people for what they are.

Sometimes you even have to ignore yourself. You can be your own harshest critic; I am mine.

Listen to advice, but don't be dictated to by it.

DON'T
make choices out of desperation

I'm not suggesting you're having a bad week but some of you might :(

If things are looking desperate and you're feeling completely out of control, it's tempting to 'try anything' as long as it's something.

'Anything' is not a solution.

Sometimes doing nothing is the best answer.

So 'Don't Panic!'

I have wasps in my brain!

We overthink everything.

Have I done it right? What if I've got it wrong?

Is it too much? Is it enough?

Should I start it again?

Should I tell people about it? Should I keep it a secret?

What will people think? Does it even matter?

Will they even care?

Was I too honest? Was I not honest enough?

Should I keep going? Should I quit?

Did I turn the stove off before I went to bed? Did I lock the back door? What if I can't sleep? My head hurts! My chest aches.

Ooh. I have wasps in my brain.

Remember: Worry can give a small thing a big shadow.

So 'don't worry, be happy now'.

ARTHUR LUKE

We do what we do - Until we don't!

I know it sounds obvious, but it's a powerful, simple truth *(this is page 55 so by now you will have noticed I am a man of simple truths)*.

We stay in jobs that pay poorly because jobs are scarce and we're afraid we won't get a better one. We will!

We keep on keeping on because we think we have no choice. We do!

We complicate everything. We coat simple decisions in elaborate excuses.

We believe there is no other way than to keep on doing what we're doing. There is!

No matter how trapped you feel, you do have options; they may need courage, and they may be difficult, but you do have them.

It's your life, and if you really want to change it, you have to decide to make something happen.

'You have to be the cause, not the effect'.

ARTHUR LUKE

"Beware the lollipop of mediocrity; lick it once, and you'll suck forever!" - The Beach Boys

Every day, too many of us settle for average. Who can blame us?

Average is safe. It takes no risks, it makes no waves and climbs no mountains, it goes along with the crowd, and it's invisible. But if life is about experiences and challenges then 'average' achieves nothing, all you gain is a list of 'if onlys' to look back on.

Sadly too many of us will remain the passenger instead of the driver of our lives. Nothing more than an anonymous cog in a corporate wheel.

"The masses of men lead lives of quiet desperation." Henry David Thoreau

Average is always there lurking in the background, waiting for an opportunity to take you hostage. It can come in the disguise of early success, early failures, setbacks, disappointment and a wish to find the easy way rather than the best way.

Don't fear failure, fear mediocrity.

I believe great artists, writers, musicians, inventors and companies succeed because in the beginning, at least, it wasn't failure they feared – it was mediocrity.

ARTHUR LUKE

fly?

It needs no lengthy explanation.

No fanciful theories.

No list of motivational 'guru' reasons why.

You can fly - because you can.

That dream you (we all have them) carry around every day in your head, is special, it's important, and you should do it!

As Peter Pan said *"The moment you doubt whether you can fly, you cease forever to be able to do it."*

So do it!

Don't be a prisoner of experience

Experience prevents us *(some of the time)* moving from one failure to another.

'The stumble that prevents the fall'.

But experience is a slow and misleading teacher.

Experience can set you free, but it can also make you a prisoner of the past.

Listen to it with caution as what we learn is not always what we need.

Make the obstacles of your past, the stepping stones of your future!

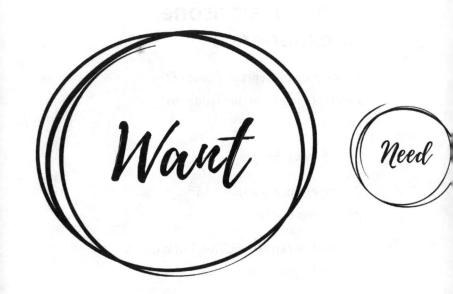

If you own less than you want, you will still have more than you need.

The other day I had to take a couple of old chairs to the city dump and when I got arrived, there was a line of cars stretching down the street, all waiting to dump stuff they no longer wanted or needed. The things they had probably paid lots of money for and at the time could not possibly live without was now worthless junk to them.

"The wisdom of life consists in the elimination of non-essentials." - Lin Yutang

WORK

live!

Don't just live to work - work to live!

All work and no play makes Jack
(or Jill) a dull, boring, stressed-out,
unfocused, unfit, anti-social, pain in
the ****.

Most of us have to work to live, it's
a fact of life, but don't let your work
become your life.

Live the life you work to live for!

ARTHUR LUKE

Don't regret those things you didn't do

They're gone.

It's a waste of time, a pointless
emotion, a useless distraction.

Regret only feeds more regret.

Instead, focus on what's coming next.
And if you're waiting for something to
turn up - try turning up your sleeves
instead.

*Advice to me (and you) -
Do something you love and are
passionate about. Most (but not all of
us) don't.

The truth is...

Telling yourself the truth can be the hardest thing of all.

Tell yourself it's easy to tell yourself the truth and you're already telling yourself a lie.

You can lie to yourself with impunity. No one will find out, no one cares, and we can always call it an excuse.

The 'excuse' is our 'get out of jail free' card. It's always there in our pocket ready to save the day 'because we'd rather tell ourselves that we made a good decision than to live with the feeling that we didn't'.

"I'm starting with the man in the mirror

I'm asking him to change his ways

And no message could have been any clearer

If you want to make the world a better place

Take a look at yourself, and then make a change" - Michael Jackson

The truth has to start with YOU.

When all is said and done, more is said than done

That's all I'm saying.

ARTHUR LUKE

Beware the label - set yourself free

Labels weigh us down; they hold us back, they rarely set us free.

We give them to ourselves in the hope that a simple 'word' will make it come true or even stop us from doing something we don't think we can do.

Some labels can destroy us, mislead us, some make the journey too complicated, some stop us from trying altogether, some drive us forward, and some set us up to fail.

We don't need labels to define us.

They're just words.

Without labels the possibilities are endless.

ARTHUR LUKE

My name is Steve!

I'M AN ADDICT!

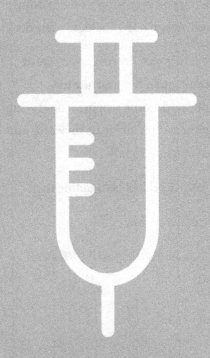

I have a good friend who has recently retired from (in his own words 'a long and bloody boring career'), so on the face of it, he now has time on his hands to do anything he wants.

He decided to learn to play the saxophone.

Within a week he had read everything he could about them, listened to YouTube 'How to' videos, read up on the history of the instrument, and he'd bought his first sax.

After two weeks he knew all the theory, he had listened to all the greats, and he was the proud owner of a beautiful and eye-wateringly expensive saxophone.

The trouble was that he couldn't play. He had done the easy bit which was driven by enthusiasm, but enthusiasm doesn't last without passion and commitment.

Within a couple of months, his sax was sitting on the shelf, an expensive trophy; he was no longer interested in learning and had moved onto something else.

As soon as the learning curve appeared, he stopped and started something else. He was addicted to starting, but starting is not enough! Being addicted to starting can be as bad as not starting at all!

ARTHUR LUKE

Beware the collector

Is it you?

Too often we end up collecting instead of doing.

We collect information, we over research, we overthink, we over clarify. We fill folders with stuff that we never read, never actually act on.

We read one more article, download one more ebook and sleep on it one more night.

Before we know it a month, two months, six months, a year or a lifetime has passed, and we haven't started doing.

Beware the accidental collector.

ARTHUR LUKE

TAKE ONE

Life is about taking decisions and making choices.

Decisions are progress. Indecision gets you nowhere. Decide and move forward, even if it feels like you're moving backwards.

You can always change your mind but to make no decision is paralysing. You get stuck in limbo. Everything grinds to a halt; the indecisions pile up, you get confused, you get overwhelmed.

Make that decision and move to the next. You will feel much better for it.

Looking back over my journey spanning nearly 63 years I wish I had taken this advice much sooner than I did.

"Good decisions come from experience. Experience comes from bad decisions." - Mark Twain

ARTHUR LUKE

my magic number

When I first left art school and moved to London to follow my dream of being a designer I was the only one of my close circle that didn't get a job in the first couple of weeks.

One by one they all landed good jobs. I kept thinking 'any day now it's going to be me'.

The days turned into weeks and the weeks into months.

Day after day I went for interviews. I made phone calls. I wrote letters. I even turned up to agencies and refused to leave until someone looked at my portfolio.

Out of desperation, I offered to work for free, but I still didn't get hired.

I went for eighty-eight interviews before someone said yes. I found out later I only got that one because no-one had applied except me.

What was the problem?

Why was I getting turned away over and over again?

I knew my work was good, but so was everyone's work.

I learned a priceless lesson from those eighty-eight painful, soul-destroying, confidence-crushing, humiliating interviews.

ARTHUR LUKE

It was me!

I was sabotaging myself.

I didn't think I was good enough.

I was feeding the 'pessimist in me' day after day. *(see page 25)*

The next job I went for, I did it differently.

I re-invented myself, I started believing in myself, I stopped feeling inferior, I began taking risks (I had nothing to lose), I 'punched above my weight', and I told myself I could do amazing things, but the most important realisation was 'I' would have to make it happen, no-one else could, would or should.

I told myself 'if the door keeps getting shut in my face, go in through the open window'.

Within a few years, everything had changed I was working on projects from New York to Milan, I was earning more than any of those friends I'd been so envious of.

I was now so good at re-inventing myself that I became three people with three very successful careers all at the same time (more on that later so keep reading :-).

If I can do it, you can too.

LIFE - Fear

"What would life be like if we had no courage to attempt anything." - Van Gogh

WARNING!

Don't try this at home kids!

One warm sunny summer afternoon, back in 1991, I stood on the edge of an old disused railway bridge north of Seattle, Washington and thought about jumping.

Looking down I felt the fear rising. The more I thought about it, the more frightened I became, quickly giving myself excuses why I should NOT jump.

After a matter of minutes, I made my decision and plunged (it was a very long way) down into the river below.

Let me explain.

This was not a bungee jump; part of a carefully planned and pre-tested exercise calculated to keep me safe. It was a leap into the unknown. No safety line, no paramedics on hand, no one there to take pictures to prove how brave I was.

I did not have to do it. No one was forcing me to do it, and no one cared if I did or didn't but, deep down, I knew I had to.

This was about me facing up to my fear.

That day I was walking with friends along an old railway track when we came to a beautiful bridge with a river below. As we all looked over the edge someone (I can't remember who) remarked how scary it would be to jump off!

ARTHUR LUKE

Warning: Don't try this at home kids!

I am, by nature, a worrier; I am the sort of person who checks (at least twice) that everything in the house is switched off before I go out of the front door. I DON'T take reckless risks, I usually think before I act and I have never felt the need to prove myself to others.

At the same time, however, I have always felt the need to prove myself to myself and have always 'jumped in at the deep end' in everything I do. My greatest challenge has always been overcoming my self-doubt.

"Life is an ongoing process of choosing between safety (out of fear and need for defence) and risk (for the sake of progress and growth)..." – Abraham Maslow

As we stood there, I could hear the others discussing how deep the water might be. What was at the bottom? Could they do it from sitting on the edge? Who would go first? Was there a ledge further down nearer to the water they could jump off, where it would be safer? Would they get into trouble? And whose stupid idea was it anyway?

While this was going on, I climbed onto the handrail and looked down at the river. The water was pretty clear, and I could see there were no rocks or reeds below the surface, no visible swirling currents, no boat about to drift by from under the bridge and there was a clear path to the bank.

Fear still winning the argument, I took my favourite baseball cap off my head and threw it into the river (sometimes we need a little added encouragement). That cap meant a lot to me, so even before it hit the water, I jumped off the bridge after it.

"Security is mostly superstition. It does not exist in nature, nor do the children of men as a whole experience it. Avoiding danger is no safer in the long run than outright exposure. Life is either a daring adventure or nothing." — Helen Keller

As a life-long entrepreneur, I have been on that ledge many times since. It has never got any easier or less frightening, but I have always jumped, and I have always survived and so will you.

Today I am a lot more prepared, as I have made most of the mistakes already.

We all face the same rising fear, and most of us come up with the same excuses. Leaving the safety of a full-time job – even a job you hate – is scary and let's not pretend it isn't.

ARTHUR LUKE

It doesn't even have to be your job. You may have always wanted to be in a band, sing in the choir or simply have the courage to step out from the crowd once in a while.

"You gain strength, courage and confidence by every experience in which you stop to look fear in the face. You can say to yourself; I can take the next thing that comes along. You must do the thing you think you cannot do." – Eleanor Roosevelt

It is not about being reckless or taking unnecessary risks; entrepreneurs are not reckless people, far from it. You have to be prepared to take risks as Ray Croc, founder of the McDonalds fast food empire at the tender age of 52, once said: *"If you're not a risk taker, you should get the hell out of business."*

It is about following your dream and finding a way to make that dream come true; through preparedness, and through listening to others who have made that jump ahead of you (watching, listening, and learning where you can) so that when you do make the jump you have minimised the risks as much as possible.

Whether you're a university graduate, just been made redundant, just retired or you're an overworked mother with a mortgage and can't remember the last time you had any time to yourself, you can do it if you want to.

"When I dare to be powerful, to use my strength in the service of my vision, then it becomes less and less important whether I am afraid." – Audre Lorde

Funnily enough, after I jumped off that bridge, I hung around in the water below for over half an hour until all but one of my friends had finally jumped too.

You see they all secretly wanted to and, once they had, they felt great about it and so did I. It became another life story to remember and re-tell…. and are those stories not a big part of life anyway?

ARTHUR LUKE

I'M AN EXPERT

It's official!

Why you should seek advice from those with wisdom, not just knowledge.

I got a call from a national radio station one day, they were running a programme about unusual travel destinations and asked would I like to come along to talk about space tourism?

I was an expert on the subject (their researcher said so).

The truth was I had once written a couple of articles about space travel but, as I had never been on a radio programme before, I thought "What the hell, it'll be fun. What's the worst that can happen?"

To be on the safe side, I didn't mention my upcoming radio debut to anyone I knew, including my wife and kids.

"It is better to remain silent at the risk of being thought a fool than to talk and remove all doubt of it." – Maurice Switzer

The night before I was due to go out live to the nation I thought I had better read up on the subject again as I did not want to sound like a complete idiot.

I arrived at the radio station in Central London at the appointed time, smartly dressed and looking every inch 'the expert', armed with nothing more than a sheet of hastily written notes, ready to face whatever perils and possible humiliation lay ahead of me.

In case anyone was in any doubt, they gave me a chest badge which said in capital letters 'Space Tourism Expert'.

It was official, and I had the badge to prove it.

Thankfully the show was a great success, and my pearls of wisdom were appreciated (and believed). The only embarrassing moment was when my notes (hidden on my lap) slipped under the table, and I had to get down on my hands and knees amongst the high heels and expensive shoes to retrieve it. The studio sound engineer was not impressed.

As I left the building, I made a mental note NOT to add 'Space Tourism Expert' to my CV.

When you are looking for a real expert, remember that all experts are not equal.

Sadly, there are too many people, especially online, armed with a little knowledge who call themselves experts, it can be difficult to tell the difference between the real ones and the hyperbole fuelled snake oil salesman.

I have met many people over the years who thought that as long as they knew more than the listener, they were the expert.

Is it just knowledge alone? – In which case could any quick reader with a reasonable memory become an overnight expert on any subject (space tourism included)?

Is it merely a case of knowing more than your listener?

"Knowledge becomes wisdom only after it's put to practical use." – Anon

Knowledge without hands-on experience is just facts, a set of rules, as anyone who has ever tried to work out how to do something from a manual knows.

"Knowledge is realising that the street is one-way, wisdom is looking both directions anyway."

Or is it wisdom and knowledge, knowledge applied and tested in real time, over time and lessons learned?

I believe you can't be an expert without a deep level of knowledge and experience.

"Nothing ever becomes real 'til it is experienced." – John Keats

If you don't face it,
you can't fix it

Most of us don't listen to what we need to hear.

Why not?

We have too much invested in where we are now. Change is not easy, and the truth hurts.

It is equally true in business and life. If we don't own up to it and look it in the face, you will have to look at it again tomorrow and the day after that.

Get out of your way and the future will open up to you.

ARTHUR LUKE

LIFE - Inspiration

*Advice to me (and you)
Never be afraid to start, but
you must start today, right
now!

I coulda been a contender – but I had to pay the mortgage

In July 1966 when I was nine years old, my Dad decided to pack up and move the family to Melbourne, Australia.

10,475 miles – which was nearly 10,475 miles further than I had ever been before in my life.

In those days moving to the other side of the world was a big deal. I would never see my friends, grandparents or cousins.

He said we had to sell all our toys, we could only take one suitcase each (plus a couple of packing cases for family stuff), and that was it.

So, with a wife and two young kids he risked everything in search of a new life, new opportunities and a dream. I can't overstate how important his attitude was in influencing my development as a person and lifelong entrepreneur.

He had courage by the bucketful, and I would like to think that I inherited this courage and passion for life from him.

On arrival in Australia, he took a series of odd jobs to feed the family including: second-hand car salesman, a worker in an ice cream factory (my favourite), an assistant accountant in said ice cream factory, builder and chauffeur to name but a few, before setting up his one-man business.

ARTHUR LUKE

He let nothing hold him back.

"When I let go of what I am, I become what I might be." - Lao Tzu

When he was fifteen, he lied about his age and somehow managed to get a job driving a goods truck down to London. My Grandma said he was so little that he had a big cushion under the driving seat to see over the steering wheel. He got into big trouble for that one, but it never stopped him thinking big.

He was prepared to follow his dream whatever the cost, and he did this until the day he died. It is that same courage and passion that makes an entrepreneur.

"Life shrinks or expands in proportion to one's courage." - Anais Nin

Fast forward to last week, and a chat with a young friend of mine.

We were having coffee, and he told me how he hated his job and desperately wanted to be his boss and be in control of his future.

As usual, I got enthusiastic on his behalf, I love helping budding entrepreneurs of any age, and I relished the exciting journey he had in front of him.

I carefully explained in depth how to begin his new journey, how to plan it out and how to minimise the risk.

He then said something I have heard too many times over the years from clients and friends, both young and old.

"Arthur, I hear what you're saying about risk and reward, and I want to do this... but I have a mortgage to pay".

Here was a healthy young guy, just turned thirty, his whole life ahead of him, with an excellent idea for a new business but already a hostage to his mortgage. The practicalities of everyday life had defeated him before he had even begun.

We all have rent, mortgages and responsibilities to family and friends; we can either hold this up as a reason not to follow our dreams, or we can use it to inspire us to pursue our dreams.

Sadly, no matter how much I tried to reassure my young friend, he could not make that leap of faith in himself and his abilities. He wanted the prize without the risk of pain. At his age, I would and did bite arms off for the same opportunity.

Everything you want in life has a cost, and you have to be

willing to pay it.

"I would have been a great guitar player if only….."

"I would have had my own successful business if only……."

"I would have been an amazing (?) if only."

"I coulda been a contender if only."

Just like my Dad, if I fail (and I have many times), I will fail on my terms; following my dream not someone else's how about you?

What's your 'if only.'

....

....

....

....

....

....

Dear Half-empty,
Cheer up.
The sun will come back.
Things will get better.
Keep on smiling.

Your good friend
Half-full :)

ARTHUR LUKE

THE DIFFERENCE
BETWEEN TRY
AND TRIUMPH
IS JUST A LITTLE
'UMPH'

- Marvin Phillips

When the going gets tough (and it will) and your enthusiasm takes a hit, when the passion begins to fade, and self-doubt creeps in.

When the goalposts keep moving, and there are so many tasks still to do, stop everything and remember the day you decided to start and why?

Remember the excitement you felt, remember how you wanted to tell everyone about your new fantastic idea, how the sun seemed to shine brighter that day.

Go back to that place then come back fighting.

Remember all you need is a little 'UMPH'.

ARTHUR LUKE

I want flowers!

"Normality is a paved road: it's comfortable to walk, but no flowers grow on it" – Van Gogh

Many people like taking the same road every day, sitting on the same train, next to the same strangers, standing in line for the same coffee, going through the same door of the same building and saying hello to the same people.

But it's not for everyone, and it's not for me.

What about you? And if it's not what are you going to do about it?

Call me :-)

ARTHUR LUKE

"Never look back
darling! it distracts
from the now"

Edna Mode - The incredibles

What life has taught me so far!

Over the last 62 years the things I've worried about, those 'what ifs' that have kept me awake at night, like wasps in my brain when I could have been looking at the world around me with wide eyes - never happened. They usually don't!

Those that did are now all in the past, and the past is the past.

As Edna Mode wonderfully said in Disney's 'The Incredibles' movie *"Never look back darling! It distracts from the now."*

What I love about watching kids movies (yes at the age of 62 I do, even though my daughters don't) is that life is always simple.

Things happen, and the characters move on. They don't dwell on the past; they always live in the now.

In real life, it's a lot easier said than done of course.

So if you can't afford to spend a week on a tropical island with Tony Robbins or some other 'I'm not your guru' guru, the answer is...

Watch a good Disney movie, and you may well find the answers to life for free.

ARTHUR LUKE

LIFE

Sometimes one is just not enough!

To say that I am a 'driven' person is an understatement.

The reasons behind this drive are too complicated for this story, and I would not want to spring it on you without prior warning. You would need supplies of beer and sandwiches, at the very least.

It might even lead you to question your sanity and would undoubtedly lead you to suspect mine.

That said, I will get back to the explanation at hand.

It was a time in my life when I was so busy and so driven that I became three separate people with three different careers, all at the same time. Only my long-suffering girlfriend (now my wife) was fully aware of my state of mind (or minds). Somehow I managed to fool everyone else.

I have always had more than one job at a time and have never fed from only one bowl. I think this stems from when I was a child. We lived on the wrong side of the track where even mediocrity was a wish too far. Evenings by the TV were peppered with drunken shouts from neighbours, along with the smell of urine drifting in from the public landing (we lived on the fourth floor).

I did not want to end up back there!

Fast forward to the early 80's. I was creative director of a leading branding agency when things first started to get a little out of hand. I was already working all hours, either in the studio or en route to meetings across Europe.

I had so many projects on the go at any one time that I started hiring friends (designers from other London agencies) to come and work for me in the evenings after they had finished for the day.

At around 11 pm I would get a cab home, go to sleep and be picked up again at 6.30am to prepare the next presentation in time for my first client meeting of the morning.

Then, one day, I had a big client presentation to prepare for. It was Friday afternoon and the illustrator I had commissioned to do some visuals let me down badly. I was two days away from the presentation with no presentation.

That weekend I decided to do his work myself and had the eight illustrations finished and ready to roll by Sunday night.

Catastrophe successfully avoided.

However, the devil was beginning to stir.

The client loved the illustrations so much that he commissioned another 15. That same week I got a call from another designer friend who had been let down at the last minute by the same illustrator.

What happened next took me eight years to bring to a close.

I found myself saying aloud down the phone "I know an illustrator who could do it! He has just done some work for me in the same style, and I'll send copies over by cab'. 'What's his name?' she asked, and, after a long silence, I heard myself say 'Mick Moscovitch'.

Mick Moscovitch was born, and to this day I don't know how I came up with the name, but he went on to have a very successful career of his own.

At his peak, he was earning more than me, and I was making a lot.

Apart from commissions for my clients and me, Mick started working for other design and ad agencies. He did work for a lot of famous publishing houses and magazines. During that time no one ever actually met Mick. His work was always delivered and collected by cab.

ARTHUR LUKE

Our home in Islington had an answering machine which took messages for my girlfriend, myself and Mick. Her friends started asking if she was living with two guys.

One day I decided it was getting too much to handle and Mick needed an agent to manage his career. As usual, I sent his portfolio to a famous illustrators agency by cab, and that afternoon I got a call from the guy who ran the agency.

He said over the phone, 'Is that Mick?' 'Yes', I said. 'Love your work, Mick, great style'.

He wanted to know more. I hesitated.

'Can I ask you about your surname?', 'Mmm OK', I said. 'Is Moscovitch Russian?' 'Polish' I said. 'Right' he said, 'but you have a Newcastle accent?'

Once again the devil took over.

'Yes I'm from Newcastle, but my parents were Polish. My father worked in the Gdańsk shipyard; they left Poland during the political troubles and moved to the Tyne to work in the shipyards there'. Completely untrue of course but it was all I could think of on the spur of the moment.

He then said the biggest piece of 'bullshit' I've ever heard in my life and the reason personality number three was born.

He said 'Yes I can see that struggle in your work. It's full of political tension.'

I put the phone down and decided to be Mick's new agent myself.

He was to be called 'Churchill Spires – illustrators agent'. He needed a name with a certain amount of gravitas. Choosing the right name, as I know from years in branding, is essential.

Before long I had other illustrator friends asking if Churchill could be their agent.

One life was not going to be enough for what I had created.

It all finally came to a head one Christmas when both Mick and I were invited to the same client Christmas party. My girlfriend sat me down and said, 'Arthur, this has got to stop, it's either Mick or me!'

He'd had a good run, he'd had a successful career, and he'd made his money, but it was time for him to retire to some desert island. I was jealous. I envied Mick.

Years later I brought Mick out of retirement, and he started his own publishing company. But I was getting too old for multiple careers and retired him again two years later.

Is there a point to this story I hear you ask?

Yes.

My point is that you don't know what you are capable of until you try.

If you're in a job or career you hate you can, with a little imagination and energy, do amazing things.

If I can create three successful careers for myself all at the same time, think what you can do.

If you need any help along the way, you know where I am, and I have loads of suggestions.

By the way, if there are any Hollywood producers out there, Mick's life story would make a great movie.

He was a bit of a wild boy, he got into expensive designer drugs and other stuff for a while, started hanging out with celebrities *(pressure of success I suppose)*. We used to hang out together sometimes as we had similar tastes *(he did get me into trouble now and again)*.

I did spend a lot of time with Mick and got to know all his secrets... Forget Walter Mitty; Mick Moscovitch was the real thing, so give me a call.

I hope this inspires you to think about breaking free from whatever may be holding you back from doing what you always wanted to do but never thought you could do.

Life holds endless possibilities; it requires a little courage *(maybe a little craziness too)*.

Remember: Everything you want in life has a cost and you have to be willing to pay it.

For me, during that period of my life, the cost was nearly my sanity.

Don't sleepwalk through life - get out there and grab those opportunities by the short and curlies.

And if they don't work out at least you will have some good stories to tell, and life is nothing more than a story, and you are the one writing it.

Recipe for life!

1. Take a cup full of passion

2. Add a measure of hope and courage

3. A spoon full of commitment and true grit

4. A drop of healthy curiosity

5. Stir in some love and affection

6. Add a pinch of '**** you' to give it some 'umph'

7. Turn up the heat, when it's hot pour it into a bowl.

Now you're ready to go!

ARTHUR LUKE

Mama told me,
there'll be days like
this!

Every Tuesday, around 6.30am, I sit down in my studio with a cup of coffee to write a weekly blog post.

Sometimes a topic will pop into my head, and off I go. Sometimes I can have 1000 words written in an hour, and I feel as if the article is bursting to get out of my head and onto my screen.

I have to be honest, most of the time it is a struggle which is why I only do one a week.

Most of the time it's like getting blood out of a stone, and that's why most people who start a blog (or anything that requires a bit of effort) give up on it, and pretty damn quickly.

Add to that the nagging feeling in the back of your mind that no one is going to read it anyway, and the whole process can often border on masochism.

Stop?

The thing is that's what most people do. They stop, or even worse, they don't even start. So why bother?

It's not as if I can't find a good excuse; we are all good at excuses, and I'm a past master.

All I can say is give yourself a chance to get there, to do it, to build it, to write it, to learn it, to say it or even to dream it.

It's on days like today when I struggle even to write the first sentence that I have to dig deep. I have to ignore the voice in my head that's saying 'go and make yourself another coffee, Arthur, write this another time'.

On days like this 'self-doubt' is there waiting, all wide-eyed and ready to take over.

What can you do? Apart from just pushing on through, here are a few things you can do to help get through days like this *(no matter what it is you're trying to achieve).*

Stop making excuses

There, I said it. And 'let the truth set you free' as they say. I could end the article right here because 'that' is the bottom line.

However, just to give you a bit more encouragement, here are four more things you can do.

Don't be too impatient

Too many dreams, plans and goals fail because we expect too much too early, and we're not prepared for the long game.

"A genius! For 37 years I've practised 14 hours a day, and now they call me a genius!" – Pablo Sarasate

Don't waste time with things you should not be doing

I don't know about you, but I always have a 'to-do list' on the go.

In fact, I have a 'daybook' and have done one for over 30 years. I can tell you exactly what I did or was trying to achieve and what my 'to do' tasks were on any given day.

What is fascinating about these books is how specific tasks were carried forward from one day (a week and even a month) to the next and were never actually completed.

'To do' lists are fine, but, if you're not careful, they can become your worst enemy. They are too easy to add to and are a constant reminder of everything you haven't done yet.

"So often people are working hard at the wrong thing. Working on the right thing is probably more important than working hard." – Caterina Fake

Make an 'Un To Do' list and stop wasting your precious time. Every task on your list comes at the expense of something else – a new opportunity. Stop tinkering!

ARTHUR LUKE

Don't let early failures defeat you

These can be one of the hardest hurdles to jump. The truth is that failures and setbacks will happen. You can count on it, especially at the beginning; and yes, they will knock the wind out of you.

Remember it's the same for everyone. Even the world's most successful people in their field have faced failure many times yet still carried on.

One of the most common reasons we fail is that we give up too soon. We hit the wall, get de-motivated, and lose confidence in ourselves.

You have to dig deep. I have to own up here and say I have given up on many ideas that, in hindsight, still had everything going for them because either I used up too much energy and enthusiasm too early on, or I just let a few setbacks destroy my faith in what I was trying to do.

"Never give in – never, never, never, never, in nothing great or small, large or petty, never give in except to convictions of honour and good sense." – Winston Churchill

Give yourself time

One of the most common excuses (because that's all it is) for not starting anything is 'not enough time', and it's a good one.

Is that really what's stopping you from starting whatever it is you've wanted to start?

I know that when you start anything new, there are so many different priorities fighting for your time and attention it can seem as if you don't have the time.

I also know that simple as it sounds, the bottom line is that, if you don't do it it won't get done!

If it doesn't get done you settle back into doing what most other people do which is to give yourself another excuse. You become just another 'if only' person.

If you want to get there, YOU WILL GET THERE. Don't give up on yourself.

There you go – finished at last!

ARTHUR LUKE

ORIGINAL®

*You don't have to be original
to be original*

Starting something new often seems too hard to start; the result being that we don't start at all.

Why?

Because we think it must be original, we believe it must be something unique and something that's never been done before, especially if it is to be successful.

In trying to be 'original' we make our goals impossible to reach, and we give up.

As a small kid, I remember my schoolteacher rapping me over the knuckles with a ruler every time she caught me glancing at anyone else's work.

'Arthur Luke! Don't copy other people's work! If I catch you doing it again, I will send you to the headmaster'. Panic-stricken, I would sit there looking at my empty page, and my brain would seize up.

Most of the time I did know the answers, but panic would cloud the way, and I would sit there unable to think of anything at all. I have been known to hand in my exam paper with nothing but my name on it.

Which is why I failed maths four times even though, at that

time, my father was my maths teacher (but that's a story for another time).

To copy was the ultimate sin and this has been beaten into us at a very early age.

Now, if I am honest, a couple of times I was caught copying facts during a test, but only because I'd been too lazy to do my homework. On other occasions I was looking for inspiration… for something, anything, to get my pen moving and get me out of panic mode.

There is a big difference between copying and looking for inspiration or looking to improve on something someone else has already done.

Unfortunately the idea that 'copying is bad' is so ingrained that we tend to apply it to everything we do, to the point that it stops us from being creative.

As little kids we copied all the time; it was how we learned to walk and talk, but, as we get older, copying becomes something we must never admit to.

Don't let the search for originality stop you from being original.

We 'copy' all the time! It's nearly impossible not to.

What makes the difference is how we individually interpret or re-interpret, reform and reproduce what we see and what we read. It is this unique personal filter (how we as an individual understand the world) that makes what we do original, not the idea itself.

We see it, absorb it and through our individual view of the world re-invent it as something different, and hopefully better.

Apple did not produce the first computer, mp3 player or mobile phone. Facebook was not the first social media network. Google was not the first search engine.

"Even in literature and art, no man who bothers about originality will ever be original: whereas if you simply try to tell the truth (without caring twopence how often it has been told before), you will, nine times out of ten, become original without ever having noticed it." – C.S Lewis

Don't stop yourself starting by trying to be original. JUST START.

'BALLS'

that's all it took

I was only 11, it was 100°f in the shade, and I was cooling off in the river when it 'hit' me.

The river was by the camp boundary and went right on through the middle of the local golf course.

On hot weekends (which was most weekends), that's where 11-year-old 'me' hung out.

It was way back in 1968, and I lived in an immigrant camp in Australia.

One morning I was standing in the river keeping cool and watching the local golfers try unsuccessfully to get onto the green.

One golfer's ball landed right by my feet (4 foot below the surface).

Being a nice young helpful kid, I picked it up, climbed the bank and handed his ball back to him.

He didn't say thank you, he didn't say 'good job mate', and he didn't say 'here's a dollar for rescuing my favourite golf ball'.

No. He just grabbed the ball and walked off.

That was my 'very first' eureka moment.

ARTHUR LUKE

Five minutes later another golfer hit his ball into the river. This time 'no more mister nice guy'. This time I sold his ball back to him.

That day I made 10 dollars, and it went up from there, and I never looked back.

I did that every Saturday and Sunday for the next year until we returned home to England.

I was the richest (self-made) 11-year-old I'd ever met.

LIFE - Growth

*Advice to me (and you)
Most things in life are a
matter of perspective. The
moment you change your
perspective, you become a
different person.

It's right to be wrong

Don't be afraid of being wrong.

Being wrong can be the perfect result.

When you're wrong, you step into the unknown.

When you step into the unknown, anything is possible.

If you think you're right all the time you're not listening, you're not asking; you're not questioning, you're not searching - you're telling.

I know lots of people who are right all the time, smug in the knowledge that they know better, rooted in their rightness, evangelistic in their arrogance.

I'm lucky! I'm often wrong.

ARTHUR LUKE

DON'T!

Don't undervalue what you're already good at

I have reinvented myself many times in my life, but success has always come from what I was already good at.

The best advice I can give is - don't undervalue what you are already good at, just get better at it.

"No one realises how beautiful it is to travel until he comes home and rests his head on his old, familiar pillow." - Lin Yutang

Without a goal - it's difficult to score!

I know it sounds obvious.

It is even a little embarrassing to say it, but we get so caught up in life's daily challenges that we forget the simple truths.

We are too busy making everything 'complicated'.

But don't you have to set goals?

Yes, and no!

I've lost count of the number of articles and quotes I have read (and I'm sure you have too) telling us that without setting goals we are doomed to failure. Now that I mention it, I remember writing a few articles like that myself.

Yes.

Yes, goals give you something to aim for, something to plan for and something to judge your progress by.

Yes, setting goals makes us feel good. They energise us and motivate us, and without them, we may as well drift aimlessly through life.

ARTHUR LUKE

Yes, it's tempting to think that if we could only map it all out so the journey ahead is crystal clear and it's in a 'to do list', then it's a matter of doing them and success will be ours!

No.

Too many goals and you don't know which one to aim at first.

Trying to plan our day, week, month or even the rest of our lives can be a bad thing!

It may look good on paper, you may even feel energised and fuelled up to go for a while, but the very same set of goals can set you back.

Continually setting goals guarantees nothing.

Too many goals especially the big ones can destroy your chances of success.

Too many goals can become a chain around your neck, reminding you of what you have not achieved, and the tasks you have not completed but said you would.

Much of the stress that we feel doesn't come from having too much to do. It comes from not finishing what we start.

*"Nothing in this world can take
the place of persistence. Talent will
not; nothing is more common than
unsuccessful men with talent. Genius
will not; unrewarded genius is almost
a proverb. Education will not; the
world is full of educated derelicts.
Persistence and determination alone
are omnipotent."* – Calvin Coolidge

ARTHUR LUKE

The man who chases two rabbits, catches neither

Be focused, stay focused, take it one step at a time.

Taking those first steps towards starting a business can be both exhilarating and paralysing. The list of tasks ahead of you can be overwhelming.

The mountain looks too big, the cost too high, the skills required too high and the risk too frightening.

Take them one at a time, and you will get there.

ARTHUR LUKE

drip

drip

drip

drip

drip

drip

drip

drip

drip

drip

drip

In the beginning, no one will:

- visit your new website that took so long to create,

- like that Instagram post, you spent so long thinking about,

- read that blog article that took you so long to write,

- buy that book you've just published on Amazon,

- listen to that song you had to bare your soul to sing,

- sign up for that webinar everyone told you you should make,

And when they eventually do - many people still won't. But that's ok *(said through gritted teeth)*!

Take it from someone who has been there many times before.

It takes time, so give it time.

Drip drip drip and you will get there.

'THE MAIN THING'

is to keep the main thing,
the main thing

Most of us make our day way too complicated.

We give ourselves 'to-do' lists we can't possibly accomplish. We set ourselves deadlines we can't meet and goals we can't reach.

We overthink things we should not even be thinking about.

A good friend of mine is so obsessed with 'to do' lists she has them pinned all over her house - even on the shower door.

The trouble is she never actually does any of them she just gets overwhelmed, then hates herself because she is not achieving anything.

Keep it simple. You know what you have to do. Keep the main thing, the main thing.

ARTHUR LUKE

Don't confuse
motion with progress

""Beware the barrenness of a busy life"
- Socrates

It can trick you into thinking you're productive when in fact what you're doing is avoiding doing something you don't want to do!

Sometimes we're so busy being busy we achieve nothing.

How many times have you got to Friday feeling shattered and exhausted only to look back and see you hadn't done any of the things you said you'd do or wanted to do.

ARTHUR LUKE

In the beginning

it's just the

beginning!

In the beginning, it's just the beginning.

You're a name no one has ever heard, a product no one knows.

You will not get rich overnight, and the world will not be beating a path to your door in the morning.

You're probably not going to be on the cover of Time or Entrepreneur magazine, and Oprah is not going to be interviewing you anytime soon.

Come to terms with that in the beginning and you will be much more likely to succeed in the end.

ARTHUR LUKE

PREPARATION
or perspiration

Or is preparation perspiration?

I believe it's more a case of 'if you get
the preparation right, there's gonna be
a hell of a lot less perspiration'.

And you smell better too :)

Here's to a sweet-smelling tomorrow.

ARTHUR LUKE

The journey is the goal

Most of the time we're so busy chasing the result, the deadline, the success (or whatever we think we must have because we listen too much to what other people tell us we should have), that we forget the most important part - the journey.

Sadly most of the time it's not until we reach the end that we realise what we have missed along the way.

If I was 16 again instead of 63 the most important piece of advice I could give to myself would be - enjoy the ride, every little bit of it, good and bad.

More importantly, don't do it all on your own. That's what friends are for!

ARTHUR LUKE

Start with what must be done first

When you start anything new, there are so many different priorities fighting for your time and attention.

There are the things that you would like to do.

There are the things others are telling you should be done. And there are the things that must be done.

Ask yourself: *What is 'it' that is getting in the way of achieving what is essential to reaching the next step, and fix that first!*

Always start with what 'must be done' first.

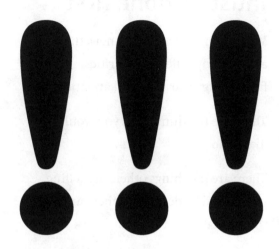

Don't let what's urgent drown out what is important.

Everything seems to be urgent.

Everybody wants to get it all done as soon as possible but when everything is a priority nothing is.

Before you know it everyone is stressed, everyone ends up chasing priorities that are not important.

If you're not careful, the important things in life, get sidelined. Family, friends, relationships and yourself.

Don't let 'urgent' drown out what is important.

Some things don't need to be done until you need to do them

Before you say 'damn it, Arthur, not another one of your ridiculous one-liners' I want to remind you (and me) that we're all masters at wasting time.

We do it every day.

We waste valuable (irreplaceable) time, energy and money (lots of it) on things that we don't need to do until we know they need to be done.

Some of these things we find out (too late) didn't need to be done in the first place.

Sometimes these even destroy any chance we have of achieving what it was we set out to do.

The trick is to know what needs to be done and when, without being distracted by all the other stuff you think (or other people tell you) needs to be done.

ARTHUR LUKE

is ok

It's where everything starts. It's the beginning of it all.

Don't be afraid of it.

Don't worry about it; it's not the end, it's only the start.

Zero is the risk you have to take to get where you want to go.

It's an excellent place to be at the beginning, because the only way from there is up.

I've been there many times, and you never stay there long.

ARTHUR LUKE

Being wrong until you are right.

Being wrong until we are right can be painful.

Who knows how long it will take?

Who knows how much it will cost?

Who knows what sacrifices you have to make along the way?

Who knows just how many mistakes it will take?

What's wrong with being wrong? Nothing!

It's how we learn. Otherwise, we never will.

Getting it wrong doesn't mean you've got it wrong.

It might mean it's not quite right yet.

It might need a tweak or two, rewording, re-emphasising, fine-tuning.

Sometimes we give up because we didn't know how close we were to getting it right.

What I am saying is… Being wrong until you are right is not always the best way to get it right.

Sometimes all you need is a guiding hand, a roadmap, a mentor, someone who already knows how to get it right.

ARTHUR LUKE

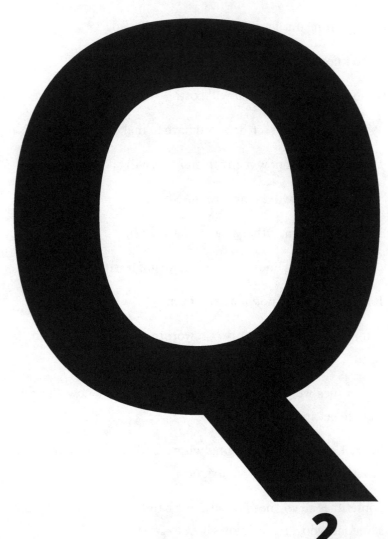

2

Life - is there more to learn from what we are avoiding, than what we are searching for?

Too often we fall into the trap of thinking the solution to our problem (whatever that is) is somewhere else.

Round the corner, over the hill, in another job, another relationship, another city, another idea, instead of fixing what we already have.

ARTHUR LUKE

Shhh!

Don't be afraid of the silence

In my spare time I sing and play in a blues band and, playing in pubs and clubs, the one thing you learn quickly is that at the beginning of your set no one is listening.

The audience is chatting with their friends, they're at the bar getting drinks, they're texting, and you're just another band.

Most of them don't care if you start playing or not.

So what do you do?

The band has two options; we can either turn up the volume, so they have no choice but to listen or leave!

Or we can dig deep, give it our best and wait for them to start listening.

Usually, it's only in the last hour of a two-hour set, and sometimes just in the last 30 mins, that their complete attention is on us (yes I know most of them are probably drunk by then and will listen to anything).

They don't clap after each song, and they don't shout out how fantastic we are – but they do turn up again at our next gig and the one after that.

ARTHUR LUKE

The next time they do clap, and they bring a friend or two.

It's the same when you start a new business, launch a new product or write a blog. In the beginning, no one is listening to you.

Don't be put off by the silence; the silence can be the hardest challenge of all.

And if you're working from home and you're doing it all on your own, the silence can be deafening.

It's scary, it's lonely, and it's what defeats most people. They get disillusioned, and they give up.

Don't be one of those people.

Keep going, silence is good; it gives you time to get it right, to test stuff, to try things and to make mistakes while no one is listening.

In the beginning, no one knows who you are; they don't know what you do or why you do it and they don't care.

That's ok. If you keep going, eventually they will.

LIFE - Failure

*Advice to me (and you)

Never be afraid to start over.
It's a chance to rebuild your
life the way you wanted all
along.

*Don't kick yourself
when you're down!*

Some days you will feel you can conquer the world before breakfast, while on other days it can feel as if the whole world has forgotten your existence and every task seems pointless.

The problem is that many of us spend too much time comparing ourselves to others; we are always judging ourselves against our neighbours, competitors, bosses, or siblings.

It's destructive, debilitating and counter-productive.

It serves no purpose other than to feed our insecurities.

It can destroy your dream before you even begin.

When we do compare ourselves with the success stories, it is too easy to forget how they claimed that success: the time it took, the mistakes and setbacks they encountered, as well as the sheer commitment and hard work they put in to get there.

Every iconic successful artist, actor, musician, entrepreneur, or writer has questioned themselves on those bleak, dark days when self-doubt, fear and uncertainty has raised its ugly head.

The difference between them and most other people is that they kept on going, they persevered and refused to give up.

We are so eager to get to where they are, or where we think

we should be, that we bite off way more than we can chew; we make rash unconsidered decisions, we let our personal lives get out of balance (we neglect our family), and our health suffers. If we are not careful, we become hostages, and ultimately, the victims of someone else's success story.

For me, these have often been difficult journeys. The learning curve is constant, the lessons are hard, but the sense of achievement and freedom is immeasurable.

So, if you feel like you're on an emotional rollercoaster, stop kicking yourself when you're down!

Here are a few things to help when things get tough.

Remember, anyone can decide to start. Those who succeed are the ones brave enough to continue and who DON'T kick themselves when they're down.

Never compare your beginning with another's middle.

Easier said than done, I know! But when you say it out loud, you realise how ridiculous it is. You have no control over 'their' journey, you don't know what their success involved, and more importantly, they are already way on down the road.

Be patient.

You are where you are, and that's OK. Accept it with grace and move forward. It takes time to achieve success.

Taking those first steps towards starting your own business can be both exhilarating and paralysing. The list of tasks ahead of you in those early days can be overwhelming; so overwhelming you can be defeated before you start.

Take it one step at a time!

Only compare yourself to yourself.

Society today continually makes us feel inadequate with our young being force-fed the notion of instant success. Everywhere we turn the media, both digital and terrestrial, seems to champion celebrity, instant success and shallow fame.

"When you are content to be simply yourself and don't compare or compete, everybody will respect you." – Lao Tzu

Compare yourself to yourself instead. Recognise how much you have achieved already, the obstacles you have already overcome. Who you are is already enough.

Celebrate don't denigrate

Don't begrudge others their success. The chances are they

have worked hard for it, and they deserve it. Don't be small minded and resentful; be open and inclusive and remember: just because someone is successful does not mean you're not!

Embrace the lows "Pain is inevitable; suffering is optional."

The author Haruki Murakami explains it like this: *"Say you're running and you think, 'Man, this hurts, I can't take it anymore. The 'hurt' part is an unavoidable reality, but whether or not you can stand any more is up to the runner himself."*

Many of us seem to relish dwelling on the negative, we waste time, energy and sleep thinking about everything that could go wrong or even will go wrong. Even in the worst situation remember most things are a matter of perspective! Change your perspective and things often look very different. A problem can be just a solution misunderstood.

Sometimes when the grass looks greener on the other side of the fence, watering the grass on your side does the trick.

Embrace the lows and recognise them for what they are, learn from them, treat them as a gift and not a punishment. Everything is figureoutable (if that's a word).

Remember there are always more opportunities.

See difficulties as opportunities and challenges as a gift. Remember that opportunities present themselves in many different forms. History is full of people who succeed against all the odds. So whether you are 16 or 66, you have a lifetime to succeed.

There is a beautiful quote by Mufasa, in the Disney movie The Lion King that goes:

"Look inside yourself. You are more than what you have become."

We are much stronger, tougher and more resilient than we give ourselves credit for.

Give yourself credit and why not?

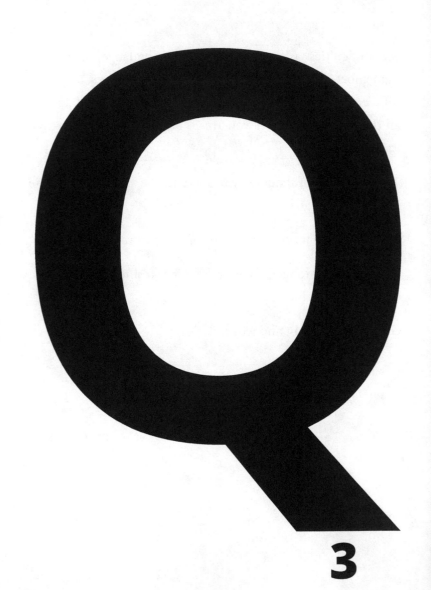

What saps our energy, wastes our time, costs us money and holds us back? What makes liars of us and stops us from being healthy, wealthy, happy and fulfilled?

A: Procrastination

How many plans and dreams have you had that you just never quite got around to starting?

Penning this, it is not my intention (if I get round to writing it), to make you feel bad about yourself. Procrastination must be one of the easiest arts to master and one which most of us are pretty damn good at.

Since I sat down to write this page, I have stopped for two cups of coffee, made some toast, read some emails, been on Facebook and, so far, I'm only here!

Our lives are littered with indecision, missed deadlines, unfinished bathrooms, unused gym memberships, unwritten novels, unfulfilled promises to friends, visits we have never made, shelves we have never put up, the list is endless.

Procrastination is a slow subconscious killer of dreams.

I read an all too familiar story in a magazine the other day it went: "When we first got married, my wife brought home a whiteboard on which we could list the jobs that needed to be done. About a year later it disappeared. Just before our silver wedding anniversary, I found the whiteboard in our garage. There were about 20 jobs on it. None of them had been done – and most of them still needed to be done".

Another story from the same article said:

"I am a teacher, I once left a set of books unmarked for so long I was embarrassed to give them back to the students yet again unmarked. So I hid them, then went into the classroom and told them they had been stolen".

Procrastination comes in many clever guises – it has fooled me many times. It can trick you into thinking you're being productive when in fact you are avoiding doing something difficult or that you just don't want to do.

We go to bed at the end of the day telling ourselves that tomorrow will be different; tomorrow we will make a start, for sure. The stage is set when we come up with more excuses for why we have not started.

"Only put off until tomorrow what you are willing to die having left undone." – Pablo Picasso

We often describe procrastination as the fear of starting something!

Maybe subconsciously we are telling ourselves 'If we don't start we can't fail'. Trouble is we will never succeed either.

"Anyone can do any amount of work, provided it isn't the work he's supposed to be doing at that moment." – Robert Benchley

So what can we do?

We could just rely on willpower, but as we know willpower is likely to let us down.

Much of the stress that we feel doesn't come from having too much to do. It comes from not finishing what we start.

Here are a few things that work for me:

Don't over think

Don't try to come up with all the reasons for why you can or cannot start. Just start. *"He who awaits much can expect little."* – Gabriel García Márquez

Set yourself realistic deadlines

Deadlines on their own are nothing more than hurdles to fall at if you don't have a clear 'do-able' plan of action to meet them.

Don't do it

Hang on – is that not procrastination again? In reality, if it's something you absolutely dread doing, then perhaps it's something you shouldn't do.

Face the fear

Fear is often the reason behind why we procrastinate. Fear can be disguised as excuses. I don't have the right tools / the knowledge / the finance / the time. I'm too old. I'm too young. It's probably been done before so I won't bother. If you don't face it, you can't fix it.

Make yourself accountable

No one wants to let their customers or their friends down, so by giving yourself a public deadline or promise, otherwise known as your 'Oh, crap!' moment', you're making it more painful and embarrassing not to finish the task.

I told everyone - the exact day I was publishing this book on Amazon (I even set up a pre-order page) before I'd even finished writing the book!

I was making myself accountable to you.

"A man who procrastinates in his own choosing will have his choice made for him by circumstance" - Hunter S Thompson

ARTHUR LUKE

Beware 'sofa' land

There's a lot to be said for just
spending the evening on the sofa but
beware!

Sofa land' is full of people with great
ideas and plans.

It's not what you plan that matters, it's
what you do that counts.

Tomorrow plans, next year plans, wait
till the kids grow up plans and wait
till I have some money plans.

Every sort of world-changing, money
making plan you could imagine.

The trouble is that's where they
usually stay on the sofa or in the
armchair.

Beware the sofa; it's where plans die.

ARTHUR LUKE

Kiss my
****

I can be lazy;

I can get disillusioned,

I can feel vulnerable,

I can be defeated,

I can feel pain,

I can lose faith,

But, when I do,

I say to that part of me

'you can just kiss my ****'.

ARTHUR LUKE

LIFE - Success

*Advice to me (and you)
"Empy pockets never held anyone back, only empty heads and empty hearts can do that" - Norman Vincent Peale

SUCCESS

never walks a straight line

It often staggers along like a drunken man.

Sometimes he falls, sometimes he stumbles backwards, but nine times out of ten he gets there in the end.

ARTHUR LUKE

It's the second mouse that gets the cheese!

Mice have moved into my studio. I can hear them scratching about in the rafters, so I set a couple of traps and what I noticed was more often than not it's the second mouse that gets the cheese.

Why repeat the mistakes of others when you can learn from them.

Someone somewhere has already been on the journey you are about to take.

That journey has given them knowledge, experience and valuable insight that could take you years to acquire on your own.

We all need mentors!

ARTHUR LUKE

go > now

Sometimes it can't be put off until tomorrow.

Sometimes you can't 'sleep on it'.

Sometimes you can't wait until it is safe.

Sometimes you can't wait for go; you have to GO.

Sometimes there is no second chance; sometimes it's now or never!

ARTHUR LUKE

'WE'
not 'Me'

I was invited to a dinner party recently and got stuck talking *(or rather listening)* to someone who bragged about themselves the whole evening.

How successful they were, how fantastic they were and how great their life was.

They learned nothing about me, they weren't interested, they didn't care, but I learned who to avoid the next time we both go to the same party.

If you want to make a difference in the world, instead of just drifting through it in your own little bubble, let your mantra be 'We' not me.

A bit more common interest instead of self-interest will take you a long way, and the world will be a better place because of you.

ARTHUR LUKE

Sometimes doing nothing is the best way forward.

If you spend a lot of time on social media, as I do, you could be forgiven for thinking that 'hustle' is everything; 'hustle is king'.

'Hustle' has become the advice du jour. The Instagrammers' mantra.

The truth is it's never all or nothing. The secret is to walk as well as run.

Working until 3 in the morning should not be seen as a rite of passage (a badge of honour) for those wanting to succeed in life.

Yes, you have to work hard to achieve success at anything but work intelligently, be 'work smart', surround yourself with people who care about you and what you are trying to do.

Seek advice from people who have already been down the road you're travelling.

ARTHUR LUKE

SUCCESS

is not somewhere else!

Success is not somewhere else!

It's not around the next corner; it's not over the next hill. It's not the next business idea.

Stop waiting for the next opportunity to come along, the next idea to appear, the next relationship, the next dream, the next bit of guru advice.

Most of the time we give up just when we are about to succeed.

It took me too many years to learn the lesson. Don't make the same mistake.

"Success is liking yourself, liking what you do, and liking how you do it" - Maya Angelou

LIFE - You

Sometimes we're so busy
listening to experts, online
gurus, celebrities, coaches,
teachers, authors, parents,
friends and the boss that we
forget to listen to ourselves.

Sometimes; we already have
the answer we're just not
listening.

'YOU'

Someone asked me recently: *'What can I do to make sure I become the best version of myself?'*

My answer was: Don't over-think it. Don't over-complicate it. Be 'you'.

You don't have to be arrogant; you don't have to shout, you don't have to pretend you're something you're not, you don't have to pretend you don't care.

Be 'you', not a wannabe celebrity, not a pretend 'guru', not a fake millionaire.

The worst thing you can do is start any relationship with a lie.

Be honest, be open, be helpful. Being 'you' is powerful and it's enough.

Self-analysis can be difficult.

Some of us beat ourselves up too much, and some of us don't question ourselves enough.

You are your most valuable asset. Protect it, nourish it, feed it and you will be perfectly equipped to make the most of it.

Being 'you' is powerful and it's enough.

ARTHUR LUKE

Just as you are!

See self-doubt and self-criticism as the bullies they are.

They pick on you when you're feeling low; they attack you when you're on your own.

They eat away at you in the middle of the night.

Deep down we don't believe we are good enough. They are those nagging voices inside our head.

Often what stops us from reaching our full potential is not lack of money, knowledge, time or opportunity, it is lack of self-belief.

Remember you are beautiful just as you are.

ARTHUR LUKE

It could be just me but...

It could be me, but I don't think so...

The person I always 'push the hardest' is me.

The person I 'always expect too much from' is me.

The person I 'always kick when he's down' is me.

The person I 'never pat on the back' after success is me.

Yes, it has driven me forward through life and helped me achieve a lot of success along the way.

Yes if I look back, I have done things I never imagined I possibly could.

But here's the thing.

If I'm honest, I could have achieved all those things and been a lot kinder to myself along the way.

If you recognise any of the above, let me tell you 'you can be kind to yourself' and still achieve everything you want in life.

So enjoy today and tomorrow and the day after that.

ARTHUR LUKE

'I'd like to be' or 'I will be'. **What's it gonna be?**

I'd like to be, or I will be!

What's it gonna be?

Because the consequences are profound.

One is merely a wish; the other is a clear decision. It requires you to take responsibility for what comes next!

'I'd like to be' sets you up for excuses not to be.

'I will be' is a line in the sand. It's a decision, and it's something you can hold yourself accountable to.

You choose. What's it gonna be?

After that, focus on what you can control; you can do no more.

ARTHUR LUKE

You could just stay in bed and leave those dreams trapped inside your head.

Get up and grab life by the short and curlies.

As Hunter S Thompson once said -

"Life should not be a journey to the grave with the intention of arriving safely in a pretty and well-preserved body, but rather to skid in broadside in a cloud of smoke, thoroughly used up, totally worn out, and loudly proclaiming Wow!"

*Beware the seller
of dreams*

They may be using you to buy theirs.

Some things never change. The snake oil salesman is alive and kicking, and he loves social media.

He's there every time you log on. He's selling quick fame, celebrity, fast cars, big yachts, wads of money, more followers, bigger dreams.

He wants to sell you the fast track to nowhere, but it's expensive and 'you must sign up for this once in a lifetime opportunity' in the next five mins, or you are doomed to a life of failure.

Sounds cynical, I know.

Yes, there are lots of good people out there who do want to help others.

They don't have an agenda.

They do have the knowledge and the experience we need. And we do all need mentors.

But remember not all experts are equal, and not all intentions are good.

ARTHUR LUKE

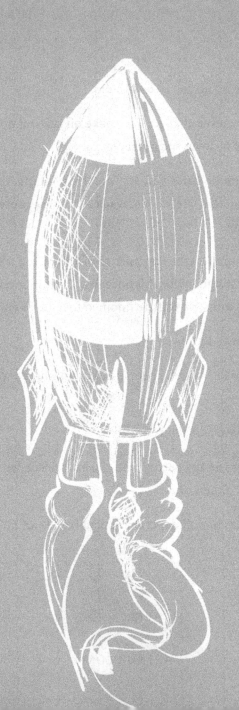

Get out of your own way!

We are masters of sabotage!

Most of the time what stops us from being who we want to be and doing what we want to do - is ourselves!

We know it but don't admit it.

We get in our way all the time. We sabotage our efforts.

We create endless obstacles and excuses. We blame circumstance; we blame others, we blame the weather.

Don't stop YOU stopping YOU.

ARTHUR LUKE

People do judge a
book by its cover

We don't want to, but we inevitably do judge everything by its cover until we know better.

Don't sabotage your new business, your new idea, product, service, book or your career by underestimating the power of first impressions.

We never get a second chance to make a first impression.

I'm a eleutheromaniac!

You can be one without even leaving
your chair.

Are you a closet one?

Are you a 'badge wearing' one?

Are you an 'anti' one?

Sometimes I am, sometimes I'm not.

Sometimes it's a good thing, and
sometimes it's not!

ARTHUR LUKE

SOMETIMES

you have to walk away

Sometimes Mondays are the best days!

Mondays can be the beginning of something good or the end of something not so good.

Sometimes Mondays are the perfect day to make big decisions.

Sometimes walking away from something is the only way to get where you need to go.

I'm not saying give up - Hell no!

I'm saying, sometimes you need to stop, step back and re-evaluate, re-position, re-focus, what you're doing 'right now' so that the week, month, the year ahead goes in the right direction.

Sometimes we all become blind to the right way forward.

And who can blame us, we've committed so much time, money, effort and grey hairs in the direction we're going right now.

The hard bit is knowing whether this Monday is one of those Mondays?

Sometimes all you need is a bit of honest (good) advice and a little (Laser focused) guidance to put you on the right track again.

ARTHUR LUKE

PLAY
don't be played

Here's a thought.

Life can be hard, and business can indeed be ruthless.

Some people will use you as a ladder to get where they want to go.

Some people will say yes to you when they mean no.

For some people, life is a game where others are to be played.

Don't let this stop you from doing it your way but play it with some passion, compassion, honesty and humility.

Be careful what you think you know!

We think people understand what we say.

We think people like what we do.

We think people recognise our intentions.

We think we are helping.

Sometimes we think someone likes us when they don't.

Sometimes we think someone doesn't like us when they do.

Sometimes we think, too much, and other times we don't think enough.

What we think is often our biggest problem.

ARTHUR LUKE

How many Mondays will it take?

We often pursue the wrong things in life, for the wrong reasons.

We follow careers we don't want to because our parents think we should.

We stay in careers we don't feel passionate about because the pay is good, or there's a good pension plan, or we are just waiting for the exit strategy to emerge.

We stay in jobs we hate because of misplaced loyalty to a boss who doesn't care about us and sometimes doesn't even know we exist.

We stay in jobs that pay badly because jobs are scarce and we're afraid we won't get a better one.

We think there is no other way than to keep on doing what we're doing.

We often work for 8 hours a day, 5, or even 6 days a week at something that makes us miserable: that is no way to live your life.

Many of us love what we do, and we wouldn't do anything else. We do it because we believe in what we do, we do it out of a passion for helping others, we do it for many reasons.

ARTHUR LUKE

Come Monday will you be doing something you want to do with your day? I hope so.

What about the Monday after that, or the one after that?

Very few of us get to do exactly what we want in life; 'life and work' or, in most cases, 'work and life' get in the way. Things have not changed much since our parents and grandparents were young and we still 'live to work to live'.

Most of us long for Fridays, hate Mondays and, as the years go by, slowly commute our way to retirement.

One day my daughter came into my studio and sat down on the sofa for a chat. She was eighteen years old at the time, and although she has been coming into my studio nearly every day since she could walk, on this particular day, she was in a reflective mood.

After a few minutes, she said, 'I hope I have as interesting a life as you have had'. 'In what way?' I asked. 'Well, you have done so many different things, you have lots of stories, you do what you want, and you don't work for someone else.'

I realised that for her entire life I had not had a 'conventional' day job. During that time I have never been a commuter, every project and business idea has been entirely different from the last and no two days have been the same.

What impressed me about what she had just said was that she is interested in the richness of life, and not how much money I had made, whether I had a 'cool' job title or if I would have a comfortable pension.

Hopefully, this means that when she does come to make her way in life, she won't be afraid to step out of her comfort zone.

Why do you do what you do?

For the money?

Because it inspires you?

Because you're good at it?

To help others?

As a stepping-stone to something better?

Because you think you would be no good at anything else?

Because you don't know what you want to do?

Or, is it because to do something else would risk the lifestyle you're used to and have come to depend on?

ARTHUR LUKE

Not everyone hates his or her job, and you may well love yours.

Many people out there are passionate about what they do. I know I am.

For some people it's a vocation, a calling, or something that speaks to them from the heart and money doesn't come into it.

But what about the rest?

According to a recent national newspaper survey, most people are miserable at work. Well, working for someone else is full of compromise, which usually involves you compromising.

What's the answer?

Well you could change your job

You might get more money

You might have a better chance of promotion

You might get more job satisfaction

You might even get a better work/life balance?

It depends on a lot of variables all of which are mostly out of your control.

Or you could try something different. If you always wish it was Friday then perhaps it's time for a change. Don't be just a step on your boss's ladder.

I've had many jobs in my life I did not like and a couple I have hated, but that was never a good enough reason to start my own business. If you hate your job, get another one!

Now we have all heard other people say that there is never a good time to start your own business. You will never be experienced enough; you will never have enough money behind you, your idea has been done before, blah, blah, blah. Well, I am here to tell you that is BS!

Being an entrepreneur does require passion (lots of it), hard work (lots of it), enthusiasm (lots of it), a clear vision of what you want to change in the world and a burning desire to be in control of your destiny. It's not for everyone.

If you have had an idea or a dream that you've been too afraid to do, it may be big; it may be small, don't let YOU keep YOU from giving it a try.

I love Mondays.

Full of possibilities and a whole week to try them out.

ARTHUR LUKE

Do you want milk with that?

Why, when I ask for a 'black' coffee
in a cafe, does the barista always say -
"Do you want milk with that?"

Is it because after the umpteenth order
they only remember the last thing you
said. 'Coffee'.

Or is it because life is so full of noise
these days no one listens to anyone?

ARTHUR LUKE

YOU
can't please everyone

Some people will be interested in what you have to say and some won't.

Some people will like what you do and some won't.

Some will love the way you look and some won't, and that's ok.

Over the years I've had my share of dismissers who said "I could do what you do, there's nothing to it", or "I read an article about that, anyone could do it".

In life whatever you do and whoever you are you cannot please everyone.

Don't waste your time on the ones that don't want to know. Focus on those that do.

Focus on those beautiful people who do like who you are and what you're trying to do.

Don't worry about the rest.

ARTHUR LUKE

Beware 'Guru' addiction

It's procrastination by another name.

Yes, good advice is priceless!

A good mentor can be life-changing (no question about it) but, like everything, 'too much can be a bad thing'.

Too much listening, reading too many articles, doing too many courses, watching too many webinars can make you more confused, more uncertain.

In the age of social media, it is too easy to put off, doing'.

It's the ultimate in procrastination.

You collect links to videos you never get round to watching, courses you paid for but never started, inspirational quotes you thought you needed but will never remember and articles you meant to read but probably never will.

When I was in my 20's and 30's (pre-internet) you had to work hard to seek out advice and knowledge. It involved standing for hours in a bookshop trying to find clues. It was a less complicated time; there was less choice and less guidance on hand to point you in the right direction.

Today there is too much information, too much advice, and too many gurus at your fingertips. Too much of everything, except time!

We're not learning, we're collecting

With too much information we risk becoming 'collectors' instead of 'doers'.

We watch other people's success looking for the ultimate answer, but it never comes.

As long as we're 'collecting' we convince ourselves we are getting somewhere, but we're not.

More choice brings more pressure. It becomes harder to avoid bad advice, shallow advice and misguided advice.

Everywhere we turn online entrepreneurs, coaching consultants, business strategists, Life coaches, Facebook experts, webinar masters and marketing gurus are telling us how successful they are, how many followers they have, how many millions they earn, how quickly they made it, and that we should be doing the same.

These self-professed gurus talk fast, they talk loud, they talk about 'hustle', they shout at you, they do impromptu fast talking Snapchats, live Instagram and Facebook videos while in a taxi on the way to their private jet, on the way to their next sold-out conference.

They are the rock stars of 'hustle', and they are all 'super pumped' and 'super excited' to be talking to you and they want to remind you unless you have forgotten, their new book is coming out next week so "don't forget to buy it".

It's exhausting.

All this can overwhelm and undermine us, leaving us feeling inadequate instead of motivated and inspired.

So what can you do?

Stop following 'gurus' and start taking action.

Have a bit more faith in yourself. You know more than you think you know.

Stop telling yourself you're not ready yet.

Stop 'collecting', start doing

Seek advice along the way (with the emphasis on 'along the way').

LIFE - If

*Advice to me (and you)
LIFE - has 'if' in it for a
reason. Make it count!

If you only knew!

If you only knew what you are capable of, you would be amazed!

I know so many people who have incredible talents that never see the light of day because they don't believe they have them.

Or worse because they don't believe they could be any good at them.

Imagine if we did what we are truly capable of instead of what we think we are capable of, what an incredible world that would be.

ARTHUR LUKE

what if you're doing it wrong

Getting it wrong is not the problem. We all get stuff wrong, and if you know you've got it wrong, you can put it right.

Sometimes getting it wrong is the best thing you could have done.

When you get it wrong, and you know you've got it wrong, that becomes knowledge and that knowledge becomes experience. 'You won't make that mistake again'. You solve it, and you move forward faster and more efficiently.

The big problem is when you don't know you've got it wrong. When that happens, you can't put it right, there is no knowledge learned, and no experience gained.

When you've got it wrong, and you don't know you've got it wrong, it costs you money; it eats into your life, it sends you off down the wrong track. You start doing more things wrong because you are building on something you've already got wrong.

How can you possibly get anything right when you don't know what you don't know?

Hell, that makes my brain hurt just writing it down.

ARTHUR LUKE

If you wait, all that happens is

- you get older

Some mornings I get out of bed and think 'I need to practise what I preach'.

Some days 'I put stuff off until tomorrow', and then tomorrow I put it off until the next day.

Not because I don't want to do them, I do. But they're a bit scary, a bit risky, I'd be stepping into the unknown (again), and it's easier to put it off.

All I'm doing is getting older.

"pile up enough tomorrows, and you'll find you are left with nothing but a lot of empty yesterdays." - Harold Hill

Don't put it off until tomorrow!

If you're reading this and you're much further down the road of life than you would like to be, remember this wonderful quote:

"It is never too late to be what you might have been." George Eliot

ARTHUR LUKE

"Society grows great when old men plant trees whose shade they know they shall never sit in." - Greek proverb

LIFE - The future

*Advice to me (and you)
It's all out there just waiting
for you - go and get it.

I've been down to the crossroads – and why you should too

This next piece is not for those of you who love your job, who can't wait to get out of bed in the morning and wouldn't wish to do anything else.

It's for those of you who don't know how that feels.

I play the blues harmonica, I have never had lessons and have never watched one of those 'how to play the harmonica' videos on YouTube. I was never in a band and had never, ever sung or played in public – I was way too shy for that.

I was so shy that I once drove from Covent Garden in London to a desolate stretch of the Norfolk coast (134 miles each way) after a particularly stressful meeting so that I could scream out loud (and I still couldn't). Now you know I'm really crazy.

When I was 51, my daughter put a harmonica in my Christmas stocking and from the moment I picked it up I was obsessed.

Now I could have left it there, happy to be a 'bedroom musician' playing safe in my room. Instead, four months later, I rang up the local village band and said, "Can I come along to one of your practices and if you think I am rubbish say and I will go home again". Today, three bands later, I am the vocalist, songwriter and harmonica player in the band (not THE Band obviously). We have been played on blues stations from Tennessee to BC.

My point is that the crossroads can be a scary place. People do sell their soul to the devil, but the 'crossroads' is where the magic happens.

It is where you discover who you are. It is where you find the talents and passions you never knew you had – and believe me, you do have them.

"The brave may not live forever – but the cautious do not live at all." – Richard Branson

My problem (if you can call it a problem) is that I can't stay away from the crossroads, I love being there.

Yes, it's scary, yes you are vulnerable and exposed, where there is nothing to protect you. You risk being laughed at, and it can be an open invitation for some to kick you where the sun doesn't shine, but the buzz is incredible. You do feel alive. It's a 'wake up and smell the coffee' moment.

I am a regular at the crossroads; in fact, I am here again writing my first book (now that is scary).

What if people think it's rubbish?

What if they pick the grammar apart or worse ignore it altogether. Well, the answer is – it doesn't matter one bit.

In my business career, I have met many 'successful' people over the years who were doing what they do for the money, for the exit strategy, for the buyout, because they have ex-wives to pay for, but they hated their job. I have friends who do what they do because to do something else would risk the lifestyle they are used to and have come to depend on, so they 'keep on keeping on'.

At this moment in time some of them earn much more money than me and drive a faster car and maybe live in a more expensive house – but I wouldn't trade places with any of them for a minute.

"When you are at the crossroads, and your heart loves one path and doesn't love the other, forget about which path has the money and the work, take the path you love" - James Altucher

We can all find excuses for taking the easy path, but that's not where the magic happens and what is life without a little magic?

Get on down to the crossroads and start to live your dream.

ARTHUR LUKE

How to use yours?

You may not believe me, but **you do have the world at your feet.** Always put the best one forward.

Be careful not to put one in your mouth.

Always have the courage to put yours down when the time comes.

When life gets hard, don't kick yourself down the road with them.

Always start off on the right one and not the wrong one.

Be prepared to think on them.

Don't drag them.

Put them up now and then because you will be run off them.

Even when you've one in the grave don't let them stop you.

Don't quit if they get cold.

Sometimes all you need is one in the door or under the table.

The time will come to use yours to sweep someone else off theirs.

ARTHUR LUKE

YOU & I

are the ancestors of the future

Life is fleeting and time is a thief,
blink and it's gone.

If we do only pass this way once, *(the
jury is still out on that)* don't sleepwalk
your way through the journey with
eyes half closed and a head full of
worry and doubt.

Leave no 'if only's' to look back on
and more importantly, leave behind
something worth leaving!

*"The timeless in you is aware of life's
timelessness. And knows that yesterday
is but today's memory and tomorrow is
today's dream."* - Kahlil Gibran

ARTHUR LUKE

Thank you

Thank you for reading this book. I hope you found it helpful, inspiring and maybe even uplifting.

Thank you to the following people:

Jenni Doig and Richard Ellis: for kindly and patiently editing out what would have made me look a fool and leaving in only what makes me look good.

Molly & Tess Luke: for bringing so much joy and purpose to my life.

Hilary Pearson: for sticking by me since 1983.

John (tigger) Magee: whose kindness and energy is spreading across world like an irresistible smile.

Alison Pearson, James Jarvis, Elizabeth Wallace, Paul Jackson, Raj Gill, Fiona Austin, Edwin & Jane Mitchell-Finch, Geoff Laycock, Kim Dong Uk, Lucia Palma, Aveline Clarke, Rakesh Tailor, Sonnie Cresswell, Dr Andy Williamson, David Hindin, Aidan Lee, Clare Chayes, Did Thread Collective, Parfums Clandestins, Eavanna Breen, Julie Noble, Rose Mary Mawee, Jimmy Gunnarsson, Jayne Carmichael Norrie, Kim Holbrook, Adie Regan, Christopher Rogers, Karen Phillips, Colleen Heidecker, Nnenna Kalu, Petina Watkins, Jimmy Gunnarsson, Helen McCarthy.

J9(The band) - Kev, Tony and Brian.

I especially want to thank all those beautiful people who have followed me on Instagram @luke.online over the last couple of years. You know who you are.

References

Extract from 'IF' by Rudyard Kipling (1865-1936)

Extract from The Flipside - Adam J Jackson *(page 25)*

Selected quotes by Lin Yutang -philosopher and inventor. Nhat Hanh, Hunter S. Thompson- Author, J.K. Rowling, William Arthur Ward, Maya Angelou, Kahlil Gibran, Francois de la Rochefoucauld, George Bernard Shaw, Daniel R Castro, Marcel Proust, Christopher Reeve, Robert Brault, Hugh MacLeod, Henry David Thoreau, The Beach Boys, Michael Jackson, Mark Twain, Van Gogh, Helen Keller, Abraham Maslow, Eleanor Roosevelt, James Altucher, Richard Branson, Audre Lorde, Maurice Switzer, John Keats, Anais Nin, Marvin Phillips, Pablo Sarasate, Caterina Fake, Winston Churchill, C.S Lewis, Calvin Coolidge, Socrates, Lao Tzu, Haruki Murakami, Robert Benchley, Gabriel García Márquez, Pablo Picasso, Norman Vincent Peale, Harold Hill, George Eliot.

You've got to the end of my book at
last! Thank you.

All I have left to say is '**you can't leave
it to others to believe in you, 'you'
have to do that'.**

www.arthurluke.co.uk